DRAW YOUR OWN CONCLUSIONS

VOLUME ONE:

SITRA'S JOURNEY

M.W.BENNETT

A COLORING, ACTIVITY, THERAPY, JOURNAL, STORYBOOK

DARK TRUTH IMAGINATIONS PUBLICATIONS, ATLANTA, GA

ISBN: 979-8-218-25092-8

MESSAGE FROM THE ARTIST

First, I am sincerely grateful for your support. Please know that I do not take it for granted. Welcome to the Dark Truth Imaginations universe. Understand, this is not just another coloring/activity book. You are about to embark on an exciting voyage alongside our hero.

Draw Your Own Conclusions, *volume one: Sitra's Journey* is an interactive experience. You do not have to be a child to participate or enjoy this piece of art. This book functions on multiple levels and serves several objectives. It works as a therapeutic tool for all ages. Whether you are working through anxiety, depression, self-esteem struggles, or simply enjoy a good inspirational story, this is for you.

My *brother-in-spirit*, Micah BlackLight and his queen Opie Snow play a significant role in my life. They encourage me, not just as an artist but as a human being. They are two of the most talented artists I know (and I know many). But their greatest masterpiece is their daughter, Sphynx. This book is dedicated to her.

She is not only the muse for our main character, but Sphynx planted the seed for the existence of this art. The cover of my first children's book, ***Create Your Own Path***, presented the main character, Amare, painting a staircase with a giant paint brush and climbing them, hence promoting the concept of cultivating your world using your imagination.

When Sphynx read the book, she brought something to my attention I hadn't noticed.

"I like the book," she said. "But we never actually see Amare creating his own path." *How did I miss that?* There's no moment in the book where we see Amare creating the way he does on the cover. That very instant gave birth to **Draw Your Own Conclusions**.

Two years in the making. Here it is. Enjoy.

Before we begin, I welcome you to document how you are feeling at this very moment. Whatever it is, just write it down.

It happens in the darkness of night when the streetlamps fade to black across the Zones and the world slumbers. I awaken to find the entire world transformed from beautiful vibrant hues into black and white. What happened? How?

If you're reading this, you are the person I need to help me answer these questions and correct this shift. We must bring color back to our world! My name is Sitra. What's yours? (Write your name ______________) This adventure is just as much your story as it is mine. I can't do it alone. First, let me bring you up to speed.

Beyond the mountains of the Danger Zone, across the Gulf of Perdition, past the Heightened Zone, and through the forest of the Forbidden Zone, you will eventually find the small town of Gentle Cove. That's my home. Folks nicknamed it the *Comfort Zone,* and that's how it feels to me.

LEARNING ZONE
DANGER ZONE
GROWTH ZONE
KORE MOUNTAIN
MOUNT DJEMBE'
HEIGHTENED ZONE
GULF OF PERDITION
FORBIDDEN ZONE
NEUTRAL ZONE
FEAR ZONE
COMFORT ZONE
GENTLE COVE

My parents made me promise I'd begin each day with a mindful breathing ritual. It helps calm my anxiety. Will you do it with me?

First, find a quiet place and sit in a comfortable position. Focus your thoughts on your breathing. Pull a deep breath in through your nose into your chest and belly. Then, slowly exhale through your mouth.

By giving attention to our breath, we can temporarily pull away from the outside chaos. I was taught that the extra oxygen circulating through the body encourages clearer thoughts.

Let's take another breath. This time, when you inhale through your nose, try holding it for a few seconds before letting it out through your mouth.

Pause. Now another one. With each breath, I feel a little more relaxed. How about you? Let's keep breathing for five more breaths.

Daily Journal...

DATE _______________

I'm a lot clearer now. All of a sudden, the air feels different in here. Do you feel it? There's someone else in here with me, and I sense…delight? I pop my eyes open and there's a Sprite Fairy hovering in front of me. Do you see him?

The Sprite lands in my hand and his shimmer vanishes. He emits a friendly aura. There is a connection between us, and I am unafraid.

"I'm so happy I found you," he says in a soft tone.

"Who are you?" I ask.

"I am Soca, head of the Elemental Sprites, from the Kai-Jen clan. We represent Autumn."

"Awesome," I say. "So, you all are in charge of coloring the leaves in the fall?"

"That we are, and so much more," he answers. He expels a deep sigh and pauses for a long moment. "Your parents sent me to find you."

"My parents? Are they okay?"

"They are unharmed but held captive."

"As you know, your parents protect the wielder of all psychic and cosmic energy. She is called the A'Kash Spark. The A'Kash resides in the Northeast temple of Mount Djembe."

My papa is the controller of Black Light. His power is to take darkness and use it in all kinds of ways. He can use it to create light, turn it into energy and shoot it at people, and mama told me he can use it to expose truth where there are lies.

My mama is the Snow Queen; she can make it so cold around her she creates ice and snow.

"Sitra, your parents are attuned to the spirit world," Soca continues. "Once the color of our world vanished, they knew the threat of the Jabaka was upon us."

"Jabaka? What is that?"

"Jabaka is the name of the three nations of Kore, combined. The leaders are *Ashen*, the Grand Wizard King of Pallid, *Esu*, the Enchantress and wielder of witchcraft and *Naira*, the Dragon Master; ruler of the Demon-Dragons of emotional disorder."

This hits me like a baseball bat to the face. My stomach tightens into a knot and my palms are sweaty. Soca continues.

"Individually, each leader remains unfit to successfully capture the A'Kash. But together they increase their chance of triumph. Your parents knew the day would come when Jabaka would become one and attempt to steal the world's spiritual power, draining it of its beauty and color, shifting our world's spiritual balance. Your parents were prepared.

"First, they brought out the hidden chest filled with resources to aid you on your quest."

"My quest?"

"Yes. The chest held *the box, the bowl,* and *the bag,* each containing a piece of what you will need to begin your journey. Your parents gave them to your friends."

"Wait, what? Slow down. This is too much to handle. I'm confused."

"Allow me to continue."

Help Sitra gain understanding. You decide who the three friends are and what items are in the box, the bowl, and the bag. Make sure you choose items that can help her on her journey.

NAME: _______________________

BACK STORY:

WHAT IS IN THE BOX?

NAME: _______________

BACK STORY:

____
____
____
____
____

WHAT IS IN THE
BAG?

____
____
____

NAME: _______________

BACK STORY:

____
____
____
____
____
____

WHAT IS IN THE
BOWL?

____
____
____

"Where are my friends now?"

"They're on their way."

"How?"

"The Snow Queen summoned her allies, the shape-shifting Falcon Sisters," says Soca. "Unfortunately, their abilities to transform into falcons merely lasts for an hour." *Only an hour? That's not much time.*

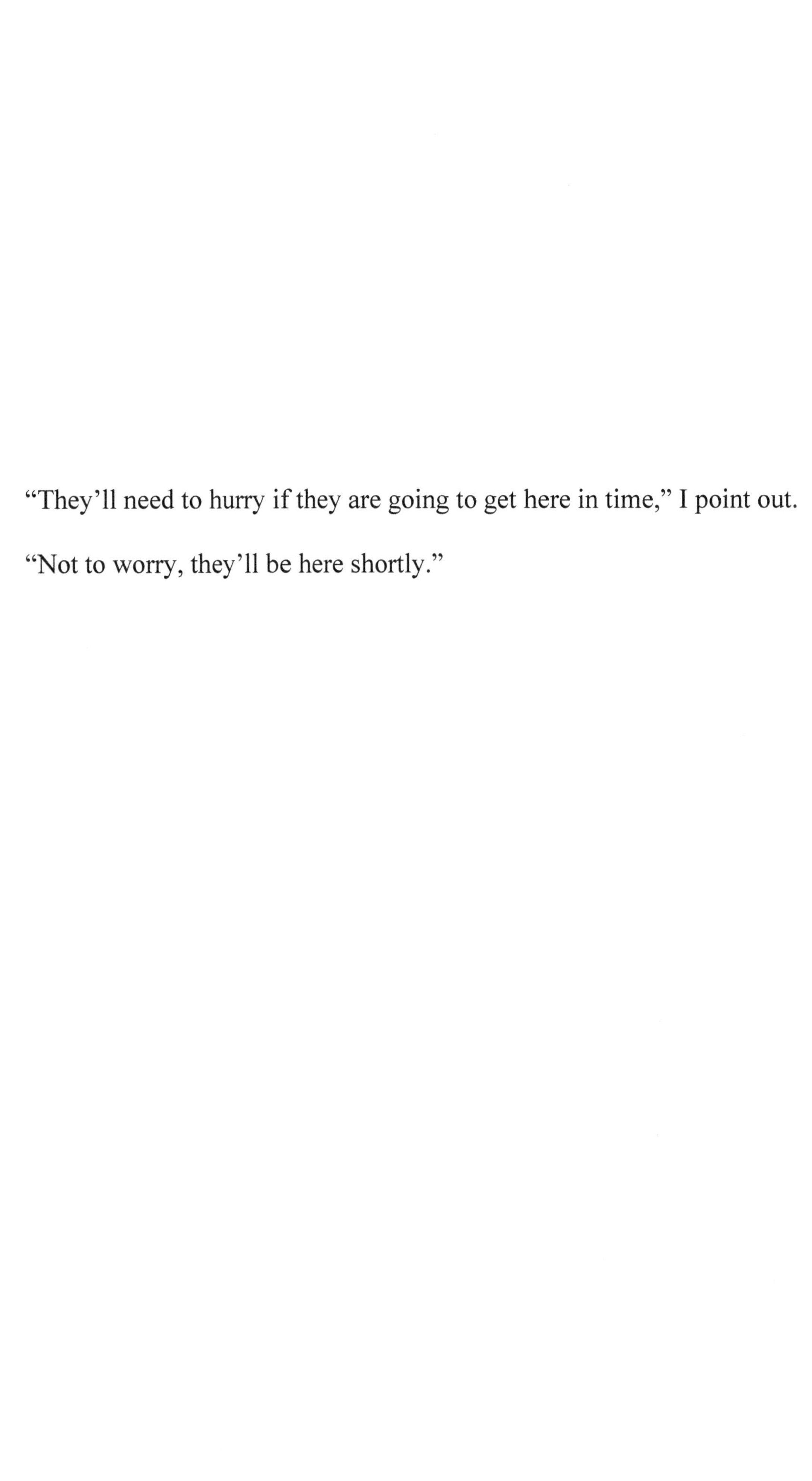

"They'll need to hurry if they are going to get here in time," I point out.

"Not to worry, they'll be here shortly."

"Your papa asked me to fly ahead to warn you."

"How did you find me?" I ask, curiously.

"He knew your mind and spirit would be open during your meditation sessions. Your spiritual light served as a beacon."

Then Soca tells me what happened to my parents. He says the Jabaka leaders descended upon the temple of Mount Djembe, mounted on one of Naira's Demon-Dragons. I can't imagine how horrific that must have been.

Soca says my parents stood their ground against the three leaders of Jabaka. But Esu the Enchantress and Ashen, the Grand Wizard combined their powers to open the mystical doorway to the spirit realm, releasing the Jumbies into our world.

"Your mother, the Snow Queen, tried to fend them off with a defense shelter made from solid ice," Soca says. "Her attempt failed."

Naira unleashed his Demon-Dragons upon my parents, capturing them.

And Ashen found the great A'Kash Spark in the Hall of Enlightenment.

Ashen encased the A'Kash in a spell of immobility, allowing emotional disorder to spread throughout the Zones.

A thud in our basement jolts my attention back to the current moment.

Stumbling down the stairs, I rush to the basement. I find my three friends waiting in the darkness, bearing the box, the bowl, and the bag. They tell me that I must leave the Comfort Zone. The first step in my mission is to find my way through the maze. That maze frightens me. My worst fear is getting lost, forever.

My friends present me with the contents of the box, the bowl, and the bag. What a wonderful set of gifts!

They say I need to find the spirits' messenger, *Moko Jumbi*.

"We must leave you now," they exclaim. "The Falcon Sisters only have thirty minutes before they transform back to their original shape!"

Back in my room, I change into my outside clothes and pull my hair into a bun, for comfort.

"How will I know how to find Moko Jumbi?" I ask Soca.

"He can only be summoned with rhythm. Sitra, you must use a drum beat to call out to him."

"But I don't own a drum."

"Then build it. Go to the forest in the Forbidden Zone with your homemade drum and play. He will find you. You can do this. I believe in you. You must be brave."

Soca's voice trails off into the distance. He's gone. Loneliness and dread weigh heavy on my shoulders. My heart feels like it's trying to burst from my chest. Deep breaths.

I need to stay grounded. I have to believe that with your help (*yes, yours*!) we can find Moko Jumbi.

Help Sitra build a *Jumbi-beckoning-drum*. If you are a kid, make sure you have adult supervision during your drum building.

Use ordinary packing tape for the drum skin. For the drum shell you can use an empty paint can or a light plastic bucket - it must be fairly strong. Apply the packing tape across the opening of the bucket diagonally, crisscrossing in an X formation. Then reinforce it with tape straight across until you have completely covered the opening of the bucket or can.

Ordinary drumsticks are fine, as are chopsticks or hardwood dowel with the ends rounded off. You can also play it by hand if you prefer.

Now you have your drum. (Good job! She's so lucky to have you as a teammate.)

She's going to need you to play your drum, later in the story.

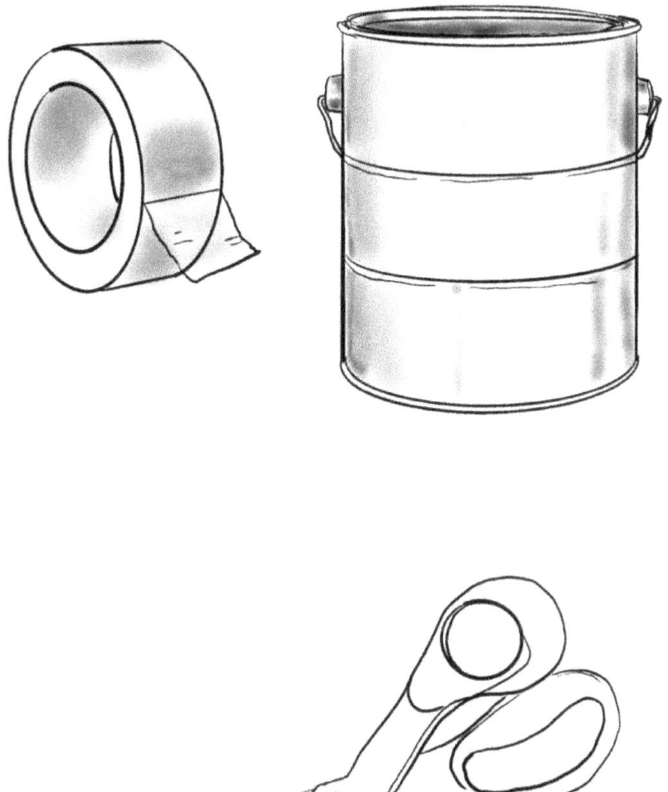

My legs tremble so badly I think they may crumble beneath me. The walls appear to grow taller the closer I get to the maze. I am fully aware this is all in my mind, but I'm still frightened.

I've never been this close to the edge of Gentle Grove or the maze before. Well, it's now or never. Walk with me?

Please, help me find my way through this maze, safely. Take as many turns as you need. We can do this together.

We made it to the other side! I couldn't have done it without you. I'm outside the Comfort Zone and entering the forest of the Forbidden Zone.

The Forbidden Zone is known to hide many dangers. I can sense five of them, but they are concealed from my sight. Can you see them? Circle the dangers so that I may pass through.

Answers:
1. Snake
2. Scorpion
3. Poisonous Spider
4. Beehive
5. Pit

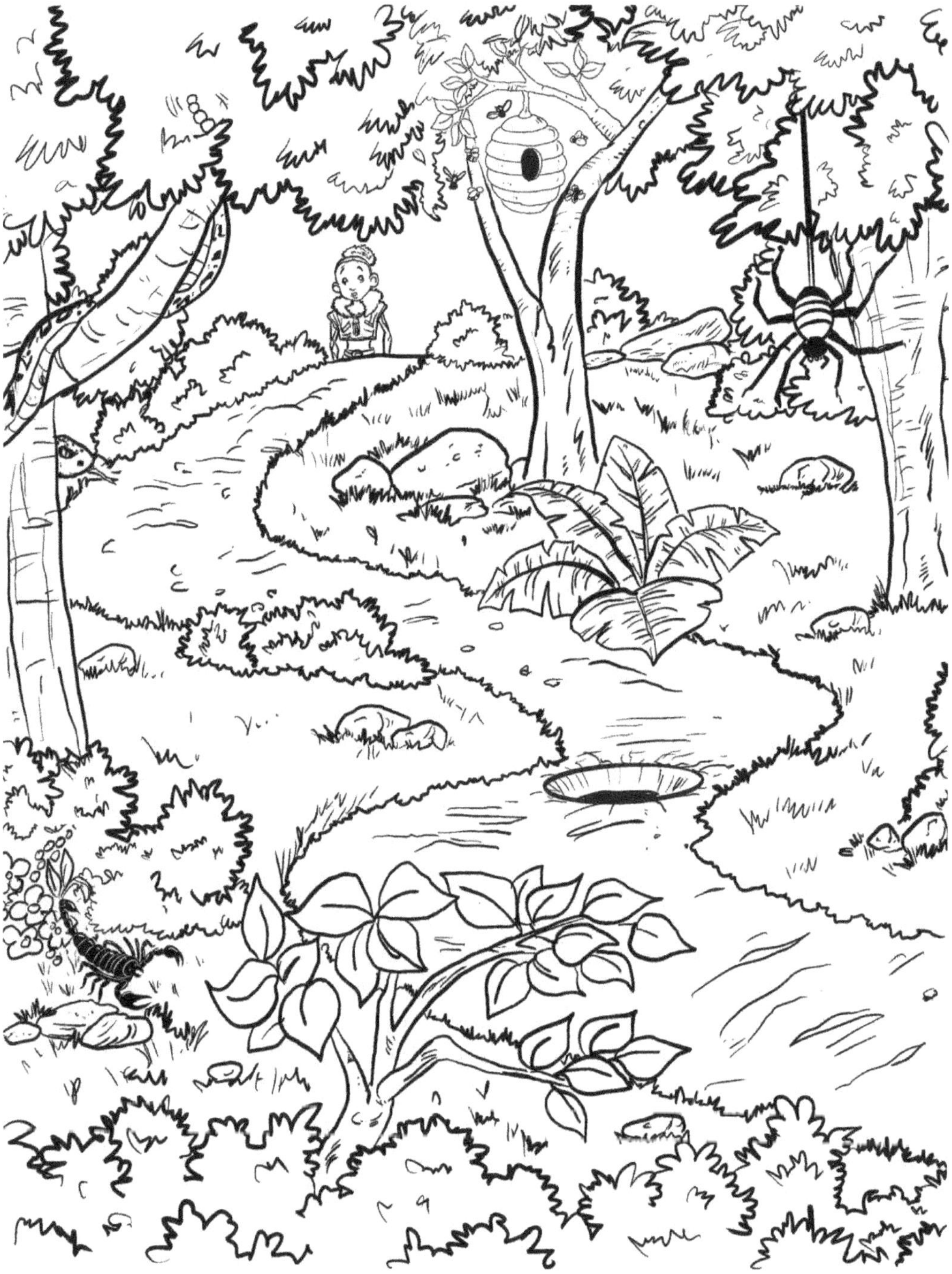

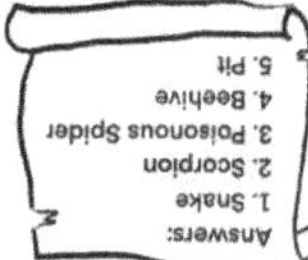

I cross over beyond the brook, exposing a wonderfully lush field where sound bounces from the trees, creating a reverberation to the heavens. I believe this to be the perfect setting to play our drum, calling out to Moko Jumbi.

After a moment of drumming, heat and light bathes the back of my neck. The crackling of an electrical surge echoes in the space around me. I turn to find a portal widening in mid-air. I stand in awe as it stretches open like a rubber band, revealing another location on the other side.

A gentle lifeforce steps through the threshold. Faceless and majestic, I can only assume he is the messenger spirit, Moko **Jumbi**. Towering above me, the creature's long legs resemble stilts.

"Under normal circumstances, little one, I'd refrain from interfering in human affairs," Moko says in a strong Caribbean accent. "But this matter is too important to ignore, as it affects both the spirit and the physical realms. Also, I sense a strong connection to the spirits in you. You are the one."

"I am the one for what?" I ask, nervously. "I still don't know what I'm supposed to do."

"First, you must find the seven crystals. Many moons ago, they were pilfered by pirates and never retrieved. They are stashed in a satchel, still deep within the hull of a sunken ship, below the Gulf of Perdition."

"How will I find the ship?"

"Here, this is a Digi-Sphere. It projects a hologram of the exact location of the ship. This will guide you."

"And these are the crystals. First, we have the ***Blood Stone*** for the Root, then there is the ***Peach Moonstone*** for the Sacral, the ***Citrine*** for Solar Plexus, ***Rose Quartz*** for the Heart, ***Blue Topaz*** for the Throat, ***Sapphire*** that enhances the Third Eye and of course, the **Amethyst** is for the Crown.

"When you find the A'Kash Spark, you must expose her to these crystals. It will re-energize her."

My hand trembles as Moko Jumbi hands me the Digi-Sphere. I place it in my belt pouch. My voice quivers when I speak.

"I'm scared," I admit.

"Remember, little one. Courage is not the absence of fear. It is moving forward despite it."

Moko Jumbi unrolls the scroll.

"These power words will give you fuel, grant you strength. They are the principles you need to assist you on your journey. However, young one, nothing in this world comes easy, eh. The words must be earned. Decode them, and they are yours for empowerment."

```
P S F V T C K D E V Z O T K K
Y Q K T C X D P V K C N S N A
S R V D R U X G O V N S R O F
L R J H E S M N L Q P H D W H
A O D T A Y T I L I M U H L D
T R C G T H C D S F L V Y E Y
S E O N I F F N I T L Q T D V
Y D U E V S K A F D O C U G R
R U R R I E H T M C E N D E O
C T A T T R Q S G P L K E K N
U I G S Y V Y R S H P Q R S O
P T E W W I J E V M Y E D C H
X A E D T C R D O Z Q Q C Y L
X R G J U E I N T E G R I T Y
D G T F S T T U S W I S D O M
```

COURAGE	INTEGRITY
CREATIVITY	KNOWLEDGE
CRYSTALS	LOVE
DUTY	RESPECT
GRATITUDE	SERVICE
HONOR	STONES
HUMILITY	STRENGTH
WISDOM	UNDERSTANDING

Moko steps back through another portal just as it nips shut behind him.

Again, I'm left isolated, accompanied only by the sounds of the distant animals and the soft rustle of leaves in the subtle breeze.

Continuing along the path, I trudge through the forest. Time passes and I hear a rumbling growl radiating from the shade behind the bushes.

I am met, eye-to-eye by a massive wolf, stepping slowly from the shadows.

Judging from the guttural growl in his throat, the look in his eyes, the drool on his chin, and the grit of his teeth, I'm guessing he is either angry, hungry, or both. I carefully step backwards. He matches my pace and marches forward.

Running is not an option. There's no way I can outrun him. The power words and advice Moko gave me seem to be working because there's no panic in me.

"Remain calm," I tell myself. "Be still."

Fangs bared and claws flexed, the wolf springs forward in a vicious attack. Yet, I stand my ground and extend my palm. Something happens. He halts in his tracks. I can feel his emotions, I sense his pain. I can interpret his thoughts. We are connected.

Across

5. The state of being uncertain; doubt; hesitancy.

6. A strong feeling of displeasure and belligerence aroused by a wrong.

7. The state of being deprived of or being without something that one has had.

8. A compelling need or desire for food.

Down

1. Characterized by or causing a depressing feeling of being alone.

2. Distress or uneasiness of mind caused by fear of danger or misfortune.

3. A distressing emotion aroused by impending danger, evil, pain, etc.

4. Lack of clearness or distinctness.

The wolf and I have a great deal in common. The second we touch; we understand one another's emotions. His name is *Vex* and I know he sees me, beyond my physical appearance. In his mind, I went from food to friend. And my perception of the wolf transformed from evil to ally.

Across
5. The state of being uncertain; doubt; hesitancy.
6. A strong feeling of displeasure and belligerence aroused by a wrong.
7. The state of being deprived of or being without something that one has had.
8. A compelling need or desire for food.

Down
1. Characterized by or causing a depressing feeling of being alone.
2. Distress or uneasiness of mind caused by fear of danger or misfortune.
3. A distressing emotion aroused by impending danger, evil, pain, etc.
4. Lack of clearness or distinctness.

I am grateful for my new friend. He grants me permission to ride on his

back, toward the oceanside. We race through the forest. He's fast.

We make it to the Gulf of Perdition. The beautiful vision across the sea makes me wonder what it might look like with color. Regrettably, I am at the end of my trek. According to the Digi-Sphere, the spot where the sunken pirate ship is located sits miles away in that direction. How do I get there?

I'm all out of ideas. Suddenly, in the grass, a door lines its way into existence, as if drawn by an invisible pen. It then becomes a real door.

Someone pops their hooded, masked head through the makeshift porthole. I don't know if they are friend or foe, but my new wolf friend stands ready to bite their head off, if it turns out to be the latter.

"I come in peace," the stranger says in a muffled voice.

"Identify yourself," The figure carefully climbs out of the hole and lowers the mask and hood. I am delighted to see my friend, Amare. In one hand he holds a pen and in the other, an oversized paint brush. We met many years ago in kindergarten. He is an amazing artist, and I am so glad he's here.

"What are you doing here?" I ask.

"You didn't think I'd let you do this alone, did you? No matter how strong, brave, or capable we are, we can all use help from a friend sometimes. Besides, in a colorless world, who better to have by your side, than an artist?"

Amare carries his tools with pride and conviction.

"Through art," he says, "we all have the ability to harness the power of magic. Art is all around us. Art has the power to change the way we see the world. It can alter the emotions of the beholder. That is true alchemy. If we master these tools and use them correctly, we can ***create our own path***. All you must do is believe. Use your imagination to craft your route to your objective."

Amare lends me his pen.

"Think about what you want and create it," he says. "Be intentional about your desires, and you can manifest them."

"What do I want?" I ask myself. "What do I need right now? Ah, I got it." Using Amare's pen, I create a rowboat, manifesting my desires through art.

"Wow," Amare says. "You are an amazing artist."

"Thank you," I reply, as we climb into the boat. Amare offers to row. I am appreciative of the gesture. Regrettably, I didn't make the boat big enough to fit Vex.

"Thank you for everything. I am grateful we met." His eyes reveal a deep sadness as Amare, and I depart the shoreline. "Bye friend. I will miss you. I hope we meet again."

The further from the shore we travel the angrier the tides become. Our boat

jostles and sways uncontrollably, as Amare struggles to retain stability. In a matter

of seconds, we find ourselves in the center of a whirlpool. We are unable to see

land in any direction. We labor to free ourselves from the massive waves. Please

help Amare steer us out of the dangerous current.

The worst is over. With your help, Amare and I made it to calmer waters. Now is the time to use the Digi-Sphere to pinpoint the exact location of the pirate ship. Amare steers the boat to the coordinates on the map.

"We are here," I say. "The prize is directly below us."

"Which one of us is going in?" Amare asks. No time for debates, I answer with action.

The coordinates instruct me to swim between the carved stones. On the left is the face of a man, and to the right, that of a lion, signifying the duality of man and beast. The lion-faced structure has six hidden divine symbols embedded within the stone siding, all of which represent *spiritual growth*. To ensure I am on the right path, find these symbols and circle them.

SANKOFA BIRD

BUTTERFLY

FEATHER

LOTUS FLOWER

BUDDHA

YIN AND YANG

Holding my breath, I swim as fast as I can while maintaining a steady pace. I try not to tire myself too soon or I'd have to come up for air. As I pass between the carvings, something changes within me. I somehow become stronger, internally, and physically.

The pirate ship comes into view in the distance. I head towards it, in hopes of finding the crystals quickly.

The Digi-Sphere directs me through the main hull of the ship. Like an eel, I

swim to the exact spot where the bag should be located. Let's hope it's there.

Thank the heavens, the crystals are here. I'm running out of air. I must move
fast.

Swimming upwards with this heavy sack proves challenging. Lurking beneath the rocks below, I sense another presence. I'm being watched. Can you see it?

Something is chasing me. I'm too afraid to look back. I can't afford to slow down. I just need to make it to the boat in time.

Exhausted and sore, I take in a hefty breath of fresh air.

“Quickly, take it!” I scream to Amare.

“Got it!” he responds. “Hurry, get in.”

“Okay.” I try to catch my breath, but it is difficult.

Something wraps around my ankle. I suck in a deep breath, just before I'm

dragged back under. Amare calls out to me, but I can no longer hear him.

This is the end for me. There is nothing I can do to escape the creature's grasp as he pulls me deeper into the depths of the ocean. I don't know how much longer I can hold my breath. There is a sudden calm to this moment. Everything around me is going black. I am at peace.

Maybe I'm hallucinating, but in the final moments of darkness, I believe I'm witnessing a school of fish, led by a mermaid, attacking the octopus. It must be true because I feel the grip on my ankle loosening. I act quickly, this may be my last chance to escape.

"What happened?" Amare asked, frantically. My lungs burn uncontrollably. It's difficult to breathe or speak. The mermaid helps me onto the boat.

"My name is Dlo," said the mermaid, in a raspy voice. "I am daughter of the sea, protector, and healer of all oceanic creatures. Alas, I was forced to discipline Shunn for attacking you. He'll be fine, though. Your mother sent me to ensure your safety."

Dlo escorts us to our destination safely. Now that the danger is gone, she's calmer and her skin tone changes. We say our goodbyes as she disappears into the ocean.

But now we are in the Danger Zone, where Jabaka resides. Their castle rests atop Kore Mountain and we need to find it if we are to rescue my parents and the A'Kash Spark. We let our instincts guide us, driven by purpose and conviction. Amare notices a pathway leading through a giant mushroom garden.

"Let's go this way."

Something is not right with these mushrooms.

Without warning, children rise bearing spears. Faceless and dirty, they exude strength, despite their small sizes.

"We mean you no harm," I say with conviction. They remain silent. Amare

dislikes the idea of spears being shoved in his face. "Stay calm," I whisper to him.

From the depths of the shadows another figure saunters between them. I imagine he is their leader.

"We are Dwens," he says. "We are the souls of children who passed prior to our spiritual shift, therefore trapped here between spirit form and flesh to protect this forest."

The leader steps so close I can smell him. I show no fear.

"I sense good in you, warrior child," he says. "You may pass. But only if you can solve my riddle."

"We have no time for games," I say.

"You have no choice. It is the riddle or the spear." No choice indeed.

"Get on with it, then." I demand. He proceeds to speak the riddle, as follows:

"You can see nothing else when you look in my face, I will look you in the eye, and will never lie. What am I?"

The Dwens permit us passage through their territory in peace. The further we walk, the thicker the air becomes. Evidently, we are close to our objective. As we cross the rope bridge and climb the small hill, we are faced with the monstrousness of Kore Mountain.

"Those rocks do not look stable enough to climb," I point out. "I can't see how we are going to make it up that mountain path." Amare smiles.

"Then we will *Create Our Own Path*," he says, holding his oversized paint brush outward like a sword.

With his magic brush, he paints stairs going up the side of the mountain.

"Fear not," he says heroically. "It is safe." Casually, we walk up the painted stairs as if they are solid. Well, the staircase is as real as the boat I drew.

Our element of surprise is compromised. In the distance, we see one of Naira's Demon-Dragons ascending from the clouds in full attack mode. He is flying straight toward us and picking up speed.

"JUMP!" Amare bellows. Missing us by inches, the Demon crashes through the homemade stairs, destroying them completely. We plummet toward the rocks below.

Amare swirls the brush and creates a slide in mid-air. I redirect my body and land on the slide at an angle to skate my way to the surface.

"He's swinging back around for another attack," Amare reports, panting. I dig into the satchel in hopes of finding something that can aid us in our time of need.

What happens next? This is **your** moment to finish the story. Use the next few pages to write and draw the completion of Sitra's Journey. This is your opportunity to guide our heroes to the completion of their mission. Do they succeed or fail? It is up to you to decide.

Draw Your Own Conclusions

(DRAW)

(DRAW)

(DRAW)

Now, share your experience. Were there any moments that stood out for you? Were you frightened for Sitra? Excited? Did you feel her growth? Did you feel YOURS?

I'm interested to see how you brought color back to Sitra's world. Please share your drawings and colors with us.

What conclusion did you come up with? I would love it if you exhibited your work on social media, as well. Let's see photos, videos, and anything else you select to display your work. I look forward to connecting with you.

If you choose to share, use the following hashtags:

#drawyourownconclusions

#createyourownpath

#sitrasjourney

Please feel free to communicate with other *create-your-own-path-PATRIOTS*. Let's interact.

Daily Journal...

DATE

Visit **darktruth22.com** for more great content.

Other books by M. W. Bennett:

Sunjata, Book One: The Blood Wars

Sunjata, Book Two: Weapons

Create Your Own Path, It All Begins in The Mind

About the author

Self-proclaimed rugged geek from Brooklyn, New York, M. W. Bennett was raised with the old Trinidadian mind-set, *"nothing is impossible and hard work equals positive results."*

He is a published author, cartoonist, painter, spoken-word performer, licensed social worker, retired Combat Army Veteran, father, and husband.